A SPY AND THE BOOK OF JOB

A Spy and the Book of Job

A Bible Study Companion for The Paris Betrayal

GARY C. HUCKABAY

James R. Hannibal

Lightraiders Press

A Spy and the Book of Job
Copyright © 2022 by Gary C. Huckabay and James R. Hannibal

Published by Lightraiders Press, a division of
XPC Media, LLC
Porter, TX, USA.
www.lightraiders.com

All rights reserved. No part of this book may be reproduced in any manner whatsoever without written permission except in the case of brief quotations embodied in critical articles and reviews.

The Paris Betrayal is a work of fiction. Names, characters, places, and incidents are products of James R. Hannibal's imagination or are used fictitiously. Any similarity to actual people. organizations, and/or events is purely coincidental with the exception of allegorical representations of the events and personalities from the biblical saga of Job.

All scripture quotations are a composite of Dr. Gary Huckabay's own translations using the following references as sources of the original language and translation for comparison:
Biblia Hebraica Stuttgartensia BHS (Hebrew Bible, Masoretic Text or Hebrew Old Testament), edited by K. Elliger and W. Rudoph of the Deutsche Biblegesellschaft, Stuttgart, Fourth Corrected Edition, Copyright © 1966, 1977, 1983, 1990 by the Deutsche Bibelgesellschaft (German Bible Society). Stuttgart.
LXX Septuatginta (LXT) (Old Greek Jewish Scriptures) edited by Alfred Rahifs, Copyright © 1935 (9th edition reprint 1971) by the Wurttembergische Bibelanstalt/Deutsche Bibelgesellschaft (German Bible Society), Stuttgart.
The New American Standard Bible NASB (NAS 1977 and NAU 1995). Copyright © 1960,1962, 1963, 1968, 1971, 1972, 1973, 1975, 1977, 1988, 1995, Lockman Foundation.
Holy Bible: New International Version, NIV. Copyright © 1973, 1978, 1984, International Bible Society.

ISBN: 978-0-578-28715-7 (printed softcover)
ISBN: 978-0-578-28716-4 (ebook)

Cover design by James R. Hannibal, jamesrhannibal.com
Interior sketch art by Marinka, Ukraine, depositphotos.com/portfolio-1006076

First Printing, 2022

The Lord gave and the Lord has taken;
May the name of the Lord be blessed.
Job 1:21b

INTRODUCTION

Will the gates of Uz prevail against us?
Two tales, two men, one story

What do Paris and the ancient city of Uz (pronounced "oots") have in common? What possible connections could there be between the fictional, modern-day character of Ben Calix, the ancient biblical person of Job, and YOU? More than you may think. Welcome to a novel (pun intended) approach to exploring real life biblical questions by comparing a fictional story, *The Paris Betrayal* (*sometimes TPB*), with the biblical saga of Job.

This is a Bible study, but we assume you have read *The Paris Betrayal*. So if you haven't, order yourself a copy and enjoy the perils of Ben Calix, a modern day Bond/Bourne spy who experiences the trials and emotional tribulations reminiscent of the patriarchal figure known as Job. Reading the entire book of Job is not a requirement. We have provided few aids in the appendices to help you navigate the seemingly endless speeches of Job and his "friends" and to help you with the study questions. The study is divided into "themes" with a Part I (the lighter version) and Part II (the deeper version). Part II of each theme contains a short commentary.

In *The Paris Betrayal,* Company agent Ben Calix returns to Paris after a rough mission in Rome involving the discovery of a potentially devastating bioweapon. His perfectly ordered world has collapsed. Attacked! Ambushed! A French SWAT team is after him. Suddenly Calix is severed from his lifelines, life's mission, and his persona, which is now cast with a non-grata class of traitors and pariahs. Was Job so different?

In the midst of celebrating life and family, Job is attacked by Sabeans! Ambushed by Chaldeans! He is crushed by the loss of his children and feeling alienated from God to the point of ripping his clothes to shreds. He declares his very birth a mistake. Will the adversaries of both stories prevail in breaking Job or Ben's spirit and loyalty? What about their faith?

Despite centuries of history separating their cultural contexts, both heroes cause the reader to consider issues of innocence, suffering, faith and loyalty, justice and injustice, friendship, man's and God's sovereignty, vindication, death and resurrection, and wisdom. In this study you can pursue these topics in a brief format with a lighter touch (Part I of each theme) or immerse yourself in the depths of Job's dialogue with his compatriots, Elihu, and God (Part II of each theme). You also have the choice to engage each topic as a single occurrence or to treat the discussions as part of an ongoing Bible study series. This can be done as an individual devotion or as a group study. For those going deeper into Job with Part II of each theme, this guide will encourage you to read pieces of the shorter Part I study first, so you don't miss some of the fruit (and nuts) of the lighter side.

The shorter study of each theme (**Part I**), is intended for book clubs or social groups, thus the title "**A Book, the Bible, and a Bit of Banter.**" The idea is to discuss the story of the book in relation to Job as if the group were a gathering of Christian pundits or maybe bloggers creating a review. In fact, we encourage individuals or groups to discuss and capture their ideas and answers in blog style and publish them on social media or a website.

The more in-depth version of each theme (**Part II**), challenges individuals and groups to use this material in a Bible study design over 12 weeks. We call Part II "**Going Behind the Gates of Uz**." In ancient times, the elders of a town would sit near the gates and discuss the important events of the day. Now it's your turn. Part II invites you to reflect on the deeper aspects of *The Paris Betrayal* and the story of Job. Each section explores a different theme. By interjecting a modern-day thriller into the study of Job, we hope to foster new and creative perspectives. The contemporary story also encourages readers to explore a variety of lifestyle applications.

HOW TO USE THIS COMPANION STUDY GUIDE

The Paris Betrayal is a tapestry of events, presuppositions, questions, and emotions with threads from the book of Job. James R. Hannibal wrote the book with the intent of entertaining his readers while challenging them to dig a little deeper into Job's spiritual dialogue and the narratives of their own lives.

This guide offers twelve studies based on twelve themes found in the book of Job, which the author was inspired to weave into *TPB*. We treat each theme separately, and each may be studied in any order by an individual or group/leader—your choice. Keep in mind, the themes complement one another, so doing them in order provides the best experience. Individuals will have no difficulty using the studies as devotionals, but we designed this companion with groups in mind.

Part I of each theme has four elements: a *starter*, an *introduction*, *story questions*, and a *Bible question(s)*. The starter question is designed to get the group thinking and talking, but don't let your discussion get caught in the quick sands of time. Treat it as what it's meant to be . . . a teaser. A short introduction of the theme follows the starter. The introduction attempts to capture the essence of the topic in a humorous or interesting modern context. Then comes the story question focused on the hors d'oeuvres of *TPB*—or cucumber sandwiches if you're having tea (I'm a "tea totaller" myself). The story questions bring out the character issues related to the theme.

A leader may want to supplement the story questions, but be careful of your time, because the meat of the theme is yet to come—the Bible study questions. In Part I, the Bible study questions broach the subject from a biblical perspective and provide a group or person something light to chew on. Part I stands alone by succinctly engaging the characters of *TPB* and Job, his friends (Eliphaz, Bildad, Zophar), Elihu, and God. But a leader may also want to refer to the commentary in Part II.

Part II of each theme incorporates Part I by referring to the starter question, introduction, and story questions found there. Next comes a *commentary* on the theme as it relates to Job and the rest of God's Word. Part II also contains more *biblical questions* and a separate section of *lifestyle application questions.*

Those who use Part I can reference the life application questions in Part II if they have the desire and the time. Like the themes in Job, the topics of each section are scattered throughout the story of *TPB*. This means **there is no direct connection to the progression of the *TPB* chapters**. For example, the loyalty of Ben emerges in various chapters and all the way to the end of the book. Thus, the individual or group should read *The Paris Betrayal* in its entirety before beginning the Bible study portion in order to fully engage each theme.

Before you begin, we suggest you pray for the wisdom to discuss some difficult subjects and take a hint from Job himself who says, "But where can wisdom be found? And where is the place of understanding?" (Job 28:1).

| 1 |

Not Me did it – "I'm innocent!"

A Reminder of How it All Works

Each theme (chapter) is divided into two parts. Part I is always *A Book, the Bible, and a Bit of Banter*, and Part II is always *Going Behind the Gates of Uz*. You're about to start Part I of Theme 1. Enjoy!

A Book, the Bible, and a Bit of Banter

Starter

Choose one character from *The Paris Betrayal* to defend as the most innocent in the story. Otto doesn't count. Who did you choose and why?

Introduction

Bill Keane, author of the Sunday funny papers' cartoon, "The Family Circus," had a favorite culprit for any accidents or cookie snatching that happened around the house. When mom or dad would ask something like, "Who ate the middle out of this cookie and put it back?"

The children would angelically reply, "Not me." Not Me was a ghostly member of the family responsible for all kinds of mayhem, while the children remained as innocent as the day they were born.

Story Questions

But were the children innocent – from the day they were born? Is anyone innocent or righteous as Job puts it? Ben Calix proclaimed himself innocent to Sensen, the sniper (p 120). Clara agreed with him (p 126). But what were Sensen's responses?

_____

_____

_____

_____

Bible Questions

Job also claimed innocence to his friends (6:24, 9:20-21). Are Ben and Job justified in proclaiming their innocence? Is "Not Me" the offender? Consider the Apostle Paul's statement in Romans 3:23 and discuss the matter of sinlessness, righteousness, and innocence. Also take a look at Genesis 15:6 and Romans 4:3, 13.

_____

_____

_____

_____

Going Behind the Gates of UZ

Starter (see above)
Introduction (see above)
Story Questions (see above)

Commentary (see the appendixes for an introduction and outline of Job)

For most scholars "the innocence" of Job is not the main theme of the story. Job's innocence or righteousness, however, is the underlying issue for the whole book. Whether or not Job's suffering is justified depends on whether or not he is innocent.

At least, that's what Job and his friends believe. How often do we find ourselves thinking something similar?

Several synonyms proclaim the hero's innocence in the book of Job. There are more English synonyms than Hebrew words but the numbers are close. These words include innocent, upright, integrity, blameless, righteous, pure, and clean. We can also include words like complete and perfect in the list.

The narrator proclaims Job's innocence right out of the gate in the first verse. Here he uses "blameless" and "upright," and he uses these again in 1:8. Eliphaz is the first to mock Job's innocence (4:7) echoing the plea from Job's own words, although Job does not use the exact term. Elihu, the last man to dispute Job, sums up the issue when he speaks. He says the others have given up because Job maintains his innocence (33:9).

Is Job blameless, without guilt? The word innocent (more like clean or pure) is not used throughout the Old and New Testaments to refer to individuals as it is with Job. The term is reserved only in reference to Christ (Luke 23:47, Hebrews 7:26). Most references are in the context evil people who would take the innocent lives of those who had done them no harm or were not a threat to them (Jeremiah 22:17). Other instances refer to the lack of innocence for a particular act of guilt or are encouragements to refrain from evil (Philippians 2:14-15).

The word innocence for Job, along with the other guilt-free adjectives, implies a complete innocence. Yet there are scholars who claim Job sinned when he challenged and denounced God for not hearing his cry. Elihu makes this argument in his speech to Job (33:12-13, 34:35-37). Is Elihu right? Did Job sin by stating his case. Is Elihu wrong and are his words full of emptiness just as he claims the other three voices are (32:11-12)? We will address this in a later theme.

To weigh Job's innocence, we must ask how we measure righteousness and unrighteousness. If Job lived in the time of the patriarchs, the law of Moses had yet to be given. In that case could Job live a life free from breaking the law since there was no law? Or do Paul's words in Romans regarding God's natural revelation apply to Job (Romans 1:18-20)? These are some of the questions that have kept biblical scholars awake at night.

Study Questions

1. Did Job claim complete innocence or just a limited righteousness beyond other men? Take a look at Job 1:1, 1:22, 2:8, 2:10, 12:4, 10:5-7, 34:36-37.

2. Was Job born without a sinful nature (Romans 5:12-13)? If not, how could he contend that he was innocent? Define innocent.

3. If we agree with Job and accept that he was innocent, how do we explain Romans 3:23?

Lifestyle Questions

1. Have you ever been punished for something you didn't do?

2. On a scale of 1 to 10 with 1 being innocent and 10 being completely guilty, where would you rank yourself and why?

3. If innocence was a garment, where would you go to purchase clean clothes (I John 1:9)?

Notes

| 2 |

Why Do the Go_d Guys Suffer?

A Book, the Bible, and a Bit of Banter

Starter

What do you see as the worst thing that happened to Ben Calix?

Introduction

No, that is not a typo in the title of this section, even if you may have thought it should read "Good Guys" or "God's Guys." You may have been influenced to substitute "Good Guys" if you read a book by Rabbi Harold Kushner entitled, *When Bad Things Happen to Good People*. It was a best seller in 1981 and was reprinted in 2004. Kushner's book inspired Christian writer and Bible teacher Warren Wiersbe to counter Kushner three years later with, *Why Us?: When Bad Things Happen to God's People*, and it was also popular.

Both authors addressed the suffering of the innocent. Kushner from a popular perspective that "good" people don't deserve to suffer (see theme #1 about innocence) and Wiersbe from the popular Christian misconception that God should shelter his people from all calamities, illness, and poverty. In *TPB*, Ben's friends assumed that he had not only stepped on his good-guy white hat, but that he'd fallen in the spy mud and become a Benedict Arnold, Robert Hanssen, or even a Judas. Ben, on the other hand, thought he'd been unjustly framed and "burned." Job's friends thought he'd crossed the line with God and was condemned as a sinner. But like Ben, Job was confused by his situation and convinced that his suffering was unwarranted.

Story Questions

Given his role in life as a government agent, should Ben have expected to suffer? What are some jobs that have similar risks for suffering?

Bible Questions

Job's friends argued that all suffering results from sinful behavior. Is that a possibility? Is it always true (James 1:2-4)?

Going Behind the Gates of UZ

Starter (see above)
Introduction (see above)
Story Questions (see above)

Commentary (see the appendixes for an introduction and outline of Job)

Anyone who has heard of the book of Job associates it with suffering. In fact, we would venture to guess that the book of Job is one of the least read books of the Bible because of the amount of suffering Job endures in just the first two chapters. Not only does Job suffer from being attacked physically but his friends add to Job's suffering (and the reader's) with endless repetition and by mockingly condemning Job for something they assume he has done. Although Job does suffer, it's interesting to note that the word is not really used in the original text. And only twice is a word associated with the toil of labor translated as "suffers." Both the Old and New Testaments struggle to find words to describe suffering except for a few cases related to the idea of carrying a burden. Job and his friends are more concerned about the cause and burden of sin than the resulting pain. They ask, "Why am I in agony?" rather than, "How much pain must I endure."

In the movie *Last Holiday*, Georgia Byrd (played by Queen Latifah), inspired by her pastor and surrounded by the church choir, bursts into a song with lyrics based on one word: "Why?" Georgia has just been told by her doctor that she has only days to live. She questions God's fairness and whether she deserves this news. Like many, she doesn't concern herself as much with the pain of death as with the reason for it.

So, why do we suffer? Here are a few reasons to consider:

1. There is sin in the world (Genesis 3:15-19). Sin in world results in calamities. When Eve and Adam disregarded God's command to leave the Tree of Knowledge alone, they brought sin upon the world. Dandelions, thistles, droughts, empty grain silos, pain in childbirth, and tornadoes are just a few of the examples of a world suffering under the oppression of sin.

2. There is sin in us. Adam and Eve were only the beginning of the suffering we bring upon ourselves (Psalm 51:3-5, Romans 5:18-19).

3. There is sin in Satan (Matthew 4:1). The first two chapters of Job demonstrate the nature of the Adversary. Read more about sin in Satan in the theme entitled "Reasonable Paranoia."

4. God disciplines those who sin against Him (Exodus 32:33-35, Acts 5:3-5). This is the premise of Job's friends. They believe that Job is not innocent but is guilty of sinning against God receiving his just reward (Job 5:17).

5. God disciplines those whom He loves (Hebrews 12:6). Like an athlete or soldier God guides our development and coaches us in the way we should walk. Sometimes this is painful, especially when we pridefully deviate from His game plan.

6. God draws us to Himself through trials (Matthew 11:28, James 1:12).

7. God prepares us through suffering to minister to others. Job's endurance has been a model and comfort for many servants of Christ (James 1:2-4, 5:11).

8. God needs no reason. In chapter 38, Job treads on thin ice by demanding God justify Himself for allowing him to suffer (see the often-quoted verse 4). SPOILER ALERT— in *Last Holiday*, Georgia Byrd had a similar experience with God when she finds out at the end that she is not sick at all and has won enough money to start her own restaurant.

Job's friends are often not wrong in their dialogue about sin and righteousness. They are just wrong about Job. Sin can draw the wrath of God as punishment or discipline calling for repentance. This was not the case with Job or with Ben Calix.

Study Questions

1. In Ben's story of suffering and Job's protest against the message of Matthew 5:45 (Job 9:22-24), are they wrong for complaining?

_____

_____

_____

2. In Romans 8:18 Paul maintains that the sufferings of his day and ours do not compare with the glory (heavenly) that awaits us. How does this impact our view of suffering, and does this imply that we are guaranteed to suffer? Take a look at I Peter 4:13 as well.

_____

_____

_____

3. Does Eliphaz (4:6-9) have a point in that we live in a universe of logical, cause and effect laws? Does sin not always result in suffering? Is suffering not always a result of sin? Is the presence of HIV in the world a result of sin? Is the COVID-19 pandemic a condemnation of world sin? Refer to Zophar's speech in 20:27 and Job's resignation in 21:23-26.

Lifestyle Questions

1. In the movie *Last Holiday*, Georgia Byrd (Queen Latifah), amidst her fellow church choir members, bursts out with the question, "Why me Lord?" Does that fit the story of Job? Or should the question be, "Why not me Lord?" See Colossians 1:24, Romans 8:16-18, and James 1:2-4.

2. Which one of the eight reasons for suffering given above in the commentary section troubles you the most? Why?

3. If God gave you the power to relieve one aspect of suffering in the world—a disease, poverty in a particular culture, an addiction, a birth defect, etc.—what would you choose to eliminate?

NOTES

| 3 |

Where's the Justice League When You Need Them?

A Book, the Bible, and a Bit of Banter

Starter

Of all the characters in *The Paris Betrayal* (*TPB*), which one would you guess was the wealthiest at the beginning? Who was wealthiest at the end? Does it matter to the plot?

Introduction

In 1959, DC Comic Books created a team of superheroes to defeat the bad guys and ensure justice—Superman, Batman, Wonder Woman, Aquaman, the Flash, Martian Manhunter (really?), and Green Lantern (my favorite and James Hannibal's favorite). Together, they and others who joined over the years fought to apprehend nefarious characters bent on causing strife and suffering and bring them to justice. Unfortunately, the real world doesn't have a group of super-wise and intuitive criminal fighters to ensure that justice is served. In fact, these days, it seems the cartels of depraved predators are thriving. Where is the justice for those who do evil?

Story Questions

Does Jupiter suffer defeat in *TPB*? Does he suffer consequences for his actions? Is there any indication that he'll be brought to Justice?

Bible Questions

In Lamentation 1:5, as Israel suffers, who prospers? What is God's purpose in this injustice? Is it an injustice?

Going Behind the Gates of UZ

Starter (see above)
Introduction (see above)
Story Questions (see above)

Commentary (see the appendixes for an introduction and outline of Job)

In the last few verses of Job chapter 11, Zophar suggests that Job is blinded by his suffering and in need of enlightenment. Job responds in 12:4-6 by acknowledging the prosperity of the marauders (Sabeans and Chaldeans) who have gained their plunder at his expense. He refers to them as "torches" (v. 5 in the original Hebrew, though found as "men" or just "he" in some translations) symbolizing power, destruction, and a life of self-indulgence (festivals). He admits that they have made a mockery of his suffering and made him a laughingstock among his friends. The unjust laugh at the just. Job goes on to give a lengthy discourse citing example after example of apparent injustice at the hand of God. These are reversals of what the just expect from life and suffering for no apparent reason. Job knows all this and agrees that the unjust prosper.

Asaph (Psalm 73) also acknowledges the prosperity of the wicked and the mockery that spreads throughout the earth (v. 9). But Asaph changes his tune in verse 17. In the temple (probably in prayer) he awakens to the truth that the unjust will receive their just reward. He awakens to his own ignorance and embraces the goodness of the Lord as his salvation—and consolation. The words of Asaph echo the feelings of many of God's faithful throughout the centuries. Each of us has questioned the Almighty and the wisdom of His ways. But the faithful always return to Him and place their trust in His lovingkindness.

So, Jupiter reminds us that crime may pay for a while, but is the ultimate payment worth it? Ill-gotten gains bring short term pleasures and give the appearance of success, but eventually the corruption of the soul pays empty dividends. There's more to be seen from Jupiter's character, which we'll see in the next segment of this companion study.

Study Questions

1. What does Asaph accomplish in the first part of Psalm 73 (1-16) by lamenting the injustice of the rich?

_____

_____

2. Was Job more worried about the loss of his family and property or that he was being mocked by his friends? Does this add to his suffering? Is Job being arrogant or self-righteous or courageous by contending for his innocence?

_____

_____

_____

3. What does the story of Zaccheus (Luke 19:2-10) teach us about Jesus' attitude toward those who have become rich at the expense of others?

Lifestyle Questions:

1. Is wealth good, bad, or ugly? Why? Take a look at Luke 16:9-13.

2. Who do you know who is richer than you? Go ahead and name names. Now ask yourself who looks at you as richer. Is this fair? Check Philippians 4:11-12.

3. Differentiate between criminal and unethical gain. Does using wealth for good justify either? Why or why not? See Mark 10:23.

| 4 |

Reasonable Paranoia – The Adversary Roams the Earth

A Book, the Bible, and a Bit of Banter

Starter

Of which movie character does Jupiter remind you: Moriarty of Sherlock Holmes, Darth Vader of Star Wars, Gordon Gekko of *Wall Street*, or Ernst Blofeld of James Bond?

Introduction

The saying "Just because you're not paranoid doesn't mean they're not after you" fits today's culture of politics, identity theft, and conspiracy theories. Recently, our church was targeted by a computer hacker who used the directory and the pastor's name to request donations for a non-existent mission in Africa. In 2006 a woman falsely accused three young lacrosse players of Duke University and destroyed their reputations as well as getting their coach fired. Despite being exonerated, the young men suffered many injustices and find their names in the news to this day.

In the story of Job, a fallen angel comes before God along with the sons of God. He goes by many names: Lucifer, Diablo, the Devil, Beelzebub, etc. On this day he is called the Satan, which means adversary or accuser in the Hebrew language. We prefer to call him the Adversary. This is a real creature, and one of the most powerful and seductive beings in the universe, be careful how you use his name.

Story Question

What was Jupiter's motive for pursuing Giselle and Ben?

Bible Questions

Why did The Adversary attack Job? Did he simply like inflicting pain on Job, or was Job a pawn in a bigger chess game?

Going Behind the Gates of UZ

Starter (see above)
Introduction (see above)
Story Question (see above)

Commentary (see the appendixes for an introduction and outline of Job)

In the book of Job the Adversary appears only in the first two chapters. He is not even mentioned in the last chapter. Although he makes a limited appearance, his encounter with God sets the context for Job's miseries. In this short commentary we by no means intend to develop a full doctrine of the Adversary. We'll focus on his intentions for causing Job's suffering. Nevertheless, his presence in the story has caused many questions and speculations about his power and relationship to God and other created beings. What was he doing "roaming" the earth? Why was he with the sons of God? Why did God allow him the ability to strike Job and his family?

Many scholars believe the "sons of God" refers to angels. They believe the Adversary fits in with them in appearance but not character. He was a prideful fallen angel. The sons of God appear again during the Lord's speech (38:7) with no reference to the Adversary. God alludes to them as holy spectators to His creative activities as they "shout for joy." The Adversary may have been one of them at that time. But in the story of Job, he did not come to praise the Lord's work. He came to claim his role as the accuser.

In the heavenly encounter between God and the Adversary (a little too civil for my taste), God first asks the Adversary where he has been. The Lord knew the answer to the question, as He did with Adam and Eve in the garden (Genesis 3:9), but by asking, He focused attention on the Adversary's actions and motives. "Roaming the earth," the shrewd serpent replied. What does that mean? What was he looking for? He was likely looking for opportunities to tempt the Lord's earthly creation to turn them against Him. The Apostle Peter warns us of the Adversary's desire to "devour" us like a lion (I Peter 5:8). In fact, Peter describes him as one prowling and walking the earth (the Greek word *peripateo* can have both meanings in that context). So it makes sense for God to ask him, "Have you considered my servant Job?"

When God tells him to consider the righteousness of Job and his faithfulness, the Adversary takes the challenge (the bait), determined to show the Lord that the only reason Job is a man faithful to God is because he is wealthy and comfortable. As the Accuser, he intends to embarrass the Lord by showing Him that His creation worships Him only for the blessings He can give them and that adversity has the power to cause them to turn their backs on Him. Like Jupiter in *TPB*, he was not interested in destroying a loyal servant . . . just his loyalty (more about this in segment V). Only then could he play his role as the Accuser.

This is not the last time the Adversary intends to turn the heart of "man." In Matthew 4:1-11, we have an account of the Adversary tempting God incarnate to sin and thus destroy God's plans for the salvation of His creation. Most, if not all of us, do not compare Christ's courage to hold his ground when tempted to Job. However, Job may be justified as a type of Christ who points to the extreme temptations of Jesus. Only Christ had the power to claim victory over the Adversary and to destroy the Accuser forever (Revelation 20:1-3).

Study Questions

1. What does Jesus mean when He says, "I was watching Satan fall from heaven like lightening" (Luke 10:17-18)? How does that relate to Job's success against his accusers? Take a look at Isaiah 14:12-13 as well.

_____

_____

_____

_____

_____

2. Read Acts 5:1-5. Did Ananias and Sapphira deserve to suffer their judgment? What was the Adversary's role in their act of greed? What would Job say about their situation?

_____

_____

_____

_____

_____

3. How does the picture of the Adversary in Job help us to be forewarned regarding the schemes of the Adversary (chapters 1-2)? Do you think Paul was aware of Job's situation when he wrote II Corinthians 2:10-11?

Lifestyle Questions

1. How does the Adversary disguise himself as an angel of light in our modern world (II Corinthians 11:14)?

2. At Caesarea Philippi, Jesus was teaching the disciples about His sacrifice when Peter took Him aside and rebuked Him, to which Jesus said, "Get behind me, Satan . . ." (Mark 8:27-33). How was Peter acting like Satan, and how do we fall into that trap?

3. Now the big question. If you met Satan on the street, how would you recognize him? Have you seen him?

NOTES

| 5 |

"Troth?"

A Book, the Bible, and a Bit of Banter

Starter

Which of these animals is considered one of the top 5 in loyalty and faithfulness—elephants, wolves, or eagles? (See the answer below in the "Starter" section of *Going Behind the Gates*)

Introduction

"Troth," what's that? In 1974-75, Dr. James H. Olthuis organized a carriage load of marriage conference notes and published, *I Pledge You My Troth*. As a young pastor searching for a cornerstone on which to build a growing ministry of pre-marital counseling, the word "Troth" piqued my interest and curiosity. Betrothed was well known to me, but what was this "troth"? It sounded a bit like something you'd find lurking in a bog. But much to my delight, it was just what I had been looking for. There on page 21 of Dr. Olthuis's book was the definition of troth and the key to lifetime commitments. "Be-trothed" means to be pledged or promised. It derives its meaning from the shorter word, troth, which means faithfulness, loyalty, trust, solemn promise, fidelity, allegiance, pledge, truth, and more. This word has more relational depth of meaning in five letters than all the words in a romance novel put together! If Job had spoken middle English, he would have proclaimed his troth to God and would have put an end to the endless speeches. For Ben Calix it should have been his Company tagline imprinted on his hat, t-shirt (front and back), and tattooed on his arm.

Story Question

Jupiter, Sensen, Hale, and Giselle all challenged Ben's troth for the Director. Which of these was most compelling and put Ben's troth at risk?

Bible Question

Can Job maintain his troth when he asks in 10:3, "Does it please you to oppress me, to spurn the work of your hands, while you smile on the schemes of the wicked?" Compare this passage with Paul's statements in II Corinthians 12:7-10.

Going Behind the Gates of UZ

Starter (see question above)

We gave you a trick question. The answer is all of them. Elephants are extremely faithful to their herd, wolves are loyal to their packs, and eagles mate for life. Dogs, of course, are considered the most loyal animals and will give their lives for their family.

Introduction (see above)
Story Question (see above)

Commentary (see the appendix for an introduction and outline of Job)

Although Job is counted among righteous men like Noah and Daniel (Ezekiel 14:14, 20), on a number of occasions he questions God as if the Lord is unfair and the cause of his sufferings (30:19-20). He laments that he is a laughingstock among his friends (12:4). Yet like the psalmist in Psalm 73, he returns in the midst of his grief to proclaim his loyalty and the wisdom and might of his Creator (12:13), exalting the God in which he has placed his faith.

In true "troth" fashion, Job declares his faith in the Lord, calling Him his "redeemer" (19:25). The word for redeemer in the Hebrew language carries with it the meaning of a family bond and faithfulness, an everlasting kinship, and a promise of redemption no matter the circumstances. Despite his constant protesting and complaining about his situation, Job remains loyal. He really never questions God's character. He only seeks His mercy and true justice. In the end Job recognizes that he didn't know God in a personal way until he sought Him in the midst of his trials. Only then could he conclude: "My ears had heard of you, but now my eyes have seen you" (42:5). Only then could he know the true comfort and confidence of God, his Kinsman Redeemer.

Job is an example for all of us. For when we see God, when our eyes are opened, we realize that it is not justice we seek but the Kinsman Redeemer, Jesus (I Peter 1:18-19). For if we were to receive justice, we would be condemned, but when our eyes are opened, we comprehend the mercy of a loving Savior who through His suffering saves us. It's His troth not ours that redeems us, and nothing can separate us from His love (Romans 8:38-39).

Study Questions

1. How does Ben Calix demonstrate his troth for the Company or the director?

_____

_____

2. Is Job being unfaithful by complaining to his friends about his pain (30:16-18)?

_____

_____

3. Was Job loyal to God? Was he faithful? Does he feel remorse in the end (42:5)?

Lifestyle Questions

1, What are the big issues of troth in a committed relationship of marriage or friendship? How might you stumble or even trample your troth?

2. What are some small, everyday ways you can demonstrate your troth in a relationship?

3. How do you repair a breach in troth with your spouse or friend? How do you do this with the Lord?

| 6 |

Friend or Unfriend?

A Book, the Bible, and a Bit of Banter

Starter

From the list of characters that follow, if you were Ben, who would you "friend" on social media and who would you "unfriend?"

Options: Sensen, Hale, Tess, Dylan/Micro, Giselle, Clara, Jupiter, and the Director

Introduction

Lucille van Pelt is bossy, opinionated, cranky, and a bully. She is arrogant and offers unprofessional advice to her friends. She loves to play practical jokes on her friends, especially Charlie Brown who trusts her over and over again not to pull the football away at the last second. You know Lucille as Lucy from the comic strip *Peanuts*. As the saying goes, "Who needs enemies with friends like her?" Job may have welcomed Lucy to his group of friends except that she would have charged him a nickel for her opinion.

Story Questions

Does Clara see Ben as friend or an assignment? What qualities make her a friend and what actions tell us that Ben is just an assignment?

Bible Questions

When Job's friends came to visit him (2:11), how do you think they intended to help him—as listeners, counselors, or religious advisors? Did their intent change?

Going Behind the Gates of Uz

Starter (see above)
Introduction (see above)
Story Questions (see above)

Commentary on the Theme (see the appendix for an introduction and outline of Job)

In *The Paris Betrayal*, Ben had to seek out his "friends." In Job's case, his "friends" came to him once they had heard of his plight (2:11). It seems they came from distant lands as indicated by their associated tribes, but no one is sure how far they traveled. The Hebrew word for friends is common in the Old Testament and used for various shared relationships. Eliphaz, Bildad, and Zophar could have been business acquaintances, extended family, or respected chieftains in nearby regions who may have negotiated peace with Job.

As they arrived, they could not believe what they were seeing and immediately demonstrated an authentic sense of mourning by tearing their clothes (2:12). This ritual is documented in ancient Egypt about 2300 BC, before the time of Job and Abraham. The dust thrown over the head is also an ancient act of contrition and symbolizes humility and a willingness to repent. These actions set the stage for the advice given by Eliphaz and his colleagues. The seven days of silence showed respect for Job's loss of family as well as for his physical condition (see also Genesis 50:10 and I Samuel 31:13). This scene of mourning is probably the first biblical account of the ritual, predating similar accounts in the Bible. Comparatively, Job is older than the others.

According to the author, Job's friends came to offer sympathy and comfort (2:11). Although they probably felt such feelings, it's also likely that they were shaking their heads (as the word for sympathy implies) in disbelief and dismay—not for Job but for themselves. If this could happen to a righteous man like Job, then this could happen to them. They were in desperate need to find out how Job brought this wrath upon himself and to assure themselves that he deserved all that he was suffering. They were probably asking themselves, "What sin was so grievous that God would bring such calamity on a man's family and on his very person?" Eliphaz reveals his thoughts when he asks, "Think about it, whoever perished who was free from guilt, and where were the upright ever wiped out?" (4:7, author's paraphrase).

Eager to vindicate themselves, Job's friends then became his prosecutors seeking to prove their case. Undoubtedly, they appealed to the onlookers at the gate using every theological gambit at their disposal. It was not that they were lying or fabricating false doctrine. Much of what they said they believed and thought would help poor Job. If he would only confess his sin. In all likelihood they held to their opinions right up until the Lord chastised them for their assumptions and prosecution of Job (42:7).

Job's friends remind us today to be careful not to be too quick to judge those caught in the throes of circumstances and calamities.

Study Questions

1. What is Eliphaz implying in 4:6 when he says, "Should not your fear [of God] be your confidence and the integrity of your ways your hope?"

_____

_____

_____

_____

2. In Bildad's initial response to Job (chapter 8), he calls him a blustering bag of wind. What does this say about Bildad's opinion of his friend's defense?

_____

_____

_____

_____

3. Zophar questions Job's wisdom and whether he can really know the mysteries of God (11:7-8). Does he have a point? Compare this to Romans 11:33.

_____

_____

_____

_____

Lifestyle Questions

1. From the moment that Job began speaking, he filled the air with emotion, sarcasm, disdain, and even vitriol. How should his friends have responded to this kind of bitterness?

2. How should we respond to someone who is hurting physically and emotionally? Listen? Sit with them? Mourn with them? Didn't Job's friends do this? Then how?

3. What should be our response to physical, financial, or family suffering when we know that it was brought on by bad decisions and immoral actions?

| 7 |

Alone in a Crowd

A Book, the Bible, and a Bit of Banter

Starter

Most animals will not abandon their young no matter the cost. Which of these is most likely to abandon their young—a horse, a buffalo, a deer, or a bear? Find the answer below in the *Going Behind the Gates of Uz* starter section.

Introduction

Shortly after our honeymoon, my wife and I arrived at our undergraduate pilot training base in the small town of Big Spring, Texas and decided to seek out a place of worship. We picked one of the 22 Baptist churches in town and were immediately invited to a Sunday School fellowship. After entering the room and surveying the situation, I left my new bride with a group of folks and went to introduce myself to a few of the men. While I was gone (just a few minutes), the group my wife was in dissipated, and she was left by herself. By the time I returned, she was beside herself and about to break into tears. "Why did you abandon me?" At first I couldn't understand. I didn't leave her in the desert or the jungle. We were surrounded by West-Texan Christians, some of the friendliest folks on earth. But for her, she was alone in a crowd and isolated from her one friend in the room, her guardian and protector for life (so much for the marriage vows). She might as well have been left with a hostile tribe of cannibals. I didn't do that again!

People can easily feel alone in a crowded room, a crowded city, and even among friends. Having a group of friends agree that they disagree with your opinion is enough make a person feel isolated and abandoned. Imagine how Job felt listening to his friends berate him for asking, "Where is my God?"

Story Question

When did Ben Calix felt more abandoned—when Sensen revealed that Ben had been "severed" as an agent (chapter 24) or when Giselle said, "You are homeless, nationless, a hunted man" (chapter 56)?

_____

_____

_____

Bible Question

Which do you think made Job feel worse—when his wife said, "Why don't you curse God and die?" (2:9b) or when he realized his friends disagreed with him?

_____

_____

_____

Going Behind the Gates of UZ

Starter: (see above for the question)

Answer: a black bear is likely to abandon a single cub because just one cub is not worth the effort of nurturing it over two years. A Panda bear will abandon a twin cub for lack of available nourishment to nurse two cubs. These facts are unbearable to think of but true.

Introduction (see above)

Story Question (see above)

Commentary (see the appendixes for an introduction and outline of Job)

The story of Job has many facets, but the facet of loneliness and abandonment is one of the most pronounced.

First, Job loses his family and property. The joy of having his children and grandchildren at hand is a great comfort to a man. Listening to their laughter and answering endless questions fills hours of empty time with great pleasure. Job had lost that.

Job also seems to have lost the companionship of his lifelong partner in marriage. Her reaction (2:10-11) to Job's circumstances suggests that she suspected him of some unrighteous act, or they wouldn't be having all this trouble. If he would only repent of whatever sin he had committed, maybe God would either restore him or at least stop tormenting him and let him die.

Then came the "stab in the back." Surely Job's wise friends would understand and bring him comfort. But to his dismay, they added to his emotional trauma. He felt alienated (19:2-4, 26:2-4). They mocked him with their words for his persistence in claiming his righteousness and for his demand to be heard in court . . . with God as his witness (12:4, 13:3). But the profundity of Job's sense of abandonment didn't stop there. It descended to the depths of Sheol, to the pit of death. He believed he was forsaken by his God (16:20-21). So he sat in the dirt, humiliated and empty, a hollow shell (14:22, 15:31).

Is Job to be pitied as the only example of someone feeling abandoned? Does not David feel forsaken (Psalm 22:1-3)? What about Paul (II Corinthians 4:8-10)? And even Jesus as He gives His life for all those who feel forsaken (Mark 15:34)? Feelings of abandonment ripple throughout the centuries, but the Lord assures us that He has not and will not forsake us even though we may abandon Him. He was with Joshua (1:9); he was with Jeremiah (1:8); he was with the apostles (Matthew 28:20); and He is with all who seek Him (Matthew 6:33).

In the end, Job's lamenting is answered by God (chapters 38-42). Job was never alone. He hadn't been abandoned, at least not by the Lord. Like Job, when we are feeling all alone, we need to seek the Almighty, but probably with a little more tact than our mentor Job. Seek Him, hear Him, see Him, and know that He is your loving Father (Matthew 6:26).

Study Questions

1. What does Job mean by saying, "I had heard you by the hearing of the ear, but now my eyes see you" (42:5)? Did he actually see God or acknowledge His presence?

2. Job's three friends condemn the unrighteous as deserving God's judgment. Is this correct coming from Eliphaz and the others? Take a look at II Peter 2:4-9.

3. God answers Job out of a whirlwind (38:1). What do you think Job felt at that moment concerning his relationship to God? What do you think Moses felt before the burning bush (Exodus 3:2)?

Lifestyle Questions

1. How should you respond to a person who says, "Go away and leave me alone?" Be sure to ask yourself if you are truly being bothersome before abandoning a person.

2. Job was really hurting, but does this justify his being impolite? How much rudeness should we tolerate when a person is distraught and being terribly disrespectful? I Corinthians 13:4-8 and Galatians 5:22-23 may offer help.

3. If Job lived in our day and age, should his friends have encouraged him to seek medical help for depression? Is that appropriate for someone who constantly wants to be left alone?

| 8 |

Choose Your God – Is It You?

A Book, the Bible, and a Bit of Banter

Starter

Who is sovereign over more land than anyone else in the United States? Jeff Bezos, John Malone, George Soros, or Donald Trump?

See the answer below in the *Going Behind the Gates of Uz* starter section.

Introduction

I am sovereign over my household and at liberty to do whatever I want . . . as long as my wife agrees. No one has complete sovereignty over their property or land. Even if you bought an island and declared yourself an independent nation, you would have to convince other nations to recognize your sovereignty. Even then, there is a small matter of the Sovereign of the universe to contend with. Individual wealth, might, political power, etc., may give the allusion of complete sovereignty, but no one can be an island to themselves and completely control their own destiny—forever.

Story Questions

Who has more sovereignty in *TPB*, the Director or Jupiter? Which of them has more sovereignty over a lightning bolt on the golf course?

Bible Question

Was Job acknowledging God's sovereignty or questioning His sovereignty? See Elihu's assessment 34:34-37 and Job's thoughts in 28:25-28.

Going Behind the Gates of UZ

Starter: (see question above in starter section)
While Ted Turner and Bill Gates own significant amounts of property, at the time of this writing, John Malone of Liberty Media is estimated to own over 2.2 million acres. If land were the measure, Mr. Malone would be king of the USA or "Maloney Land."

Introduction: (see above)
Story Questions: (see above)

Commentary (see the appendixes for an introduction and outline of Job)

In the *Star Trek* episode, "Who Mourns for Adonais," the titan Apollo claims sovereignty over his world and the starship Enterprise and its crew. He offers Captain Kirk a heavenly lifestyle if he and his crew will only accept his hospitality and revere him as their god. As was the case in other sci-fi films, the strong-willed, independent earthlings reject the sovereignty of even a benevolent god.

God's sovereignty is controversial even among Christians. The topic produces questions about human suffering, justice, judgment, natural disasters, the source of evil, the human will, and the manipulation of animals. These are not futuristic topics awaiting encounters with powerful aliens in the stars. These issues are ancient, down-to-earth matters that emerge from generation to generation. If we use a common scriptural phrase, "Lord of . . .", we may be able to catch a glimpse of God's sovereign majesty as He passes by the eyes of Job and other servants like him.

He is Lord of the stars and places the constellations in space (9:7-9).

He is Lord of the elements (Amos 4:7, Mark 4:39-41).

He is Lord of good days and bad days (Jeremiah 10:13, Matthew 5:45).

He is Lord of good deeds and bad deeds (Genesis 50:20, Acts 4:27-28).

He is Lord of life and death (I Samuel 12:6).

He is Lord of today and tomorrow (James 4:13-15).

He is Lord of our destinies (Proverbs 19:21, 20:24).

The problem Job had, as we do today, is that He IS LORD. We cannot squeeze Him into a bottle like a genie or dismiss Him as an alien with a hidden power source. He is the Creator, the Maker of all there is, and as the Almighty, He determines what is fair, what is justified, what is acceptable, what is reasonable, and what is righteous. Job affirms this conclusion in end when he says, "I know You can do all things; no plan of Yours can be thwarted." This admission lifts a burden off Job's shoulders by putting the world, and justice, back on God's sovereign and matchless shoulders.

Study Questions

1. When God speaks, He asks Job a litany of questions. What does this one in 38:4 mean: "Where were you when I laid the foundations of the earth?"

2. Is Zophar correct when he asks if Job can really know the deeper things of God (11:7-9)?

3. In Acts 4:24, in the original Greek language, the people pray to God and address Him as "despot" (the word is translated as Lord). Can a despot (one with absolute authority) be benevolent? How would you describe an earthly benevolent despot? Discuss the pros and cons of the use of this term for the Lord.

Lifestyle Questions

1. How, on a daily basis, do we challenge God's sovereignty (Romans 7:19)?

2. How do we acknowledge God's good and perfect will for our lives (Galatians 5:16)?

3. How should we respond to God if we ask Him, "Why?" and receive no answer (38:12)?

| 9 |

Repent! . . . or Not

A Book, the Bible, and a Bit of Banter

Starter

Discuss a time when the sound of your mother's or father's voice startled you because you were caught "with your hand in the cookie jar."

Introduction

I took it as a compliment, but I was dismayed one night when I happened to look out my window and see the youth group toilet-papering the front yard. I quickly put on some clothes and went out the back fence, down the alley, and snuck up behind them. The look on their faces was priceless as I said, "I appreciate your artwork, and your parents will be glad to know where you were tonight." They weren't exactly repentant, but they definitely felt remorse.

When a child is caught with a hand in the cookie jar and says, "I'm sorry," is he or she acknowledging his or her wrongdoing, or is the child simply sorry that he or she was caught? What is the difference between remorse and repentance? Did Ben Calix or Job feel a need to repent despite being accused of wrongdoing? Did they feel remorse for their situation? Remorse comes out of a sense of guilt and a regret for the consequences that follow. Remorse is the precursor to repentance which involves a change of heart and mind, and a turning or returning to a path of accepted norms (for Christians, these are biblical norms/values). Although accused again and again of a transgression, Ben and Job did not believe they needed to repent.

Story Questions

Which character in *TPB* believes Ben Calix is innocent and doesn't need to ask for forgiveness? Hint: once again, it's not Otto. What reason does this person have to believe him?

_____

_____

_____

_____

Bible Question

If anyone should have believed Job, it should have been his wife. Why do you think she urges him to turn away from God and die? See 2:9-10, and note that the word "evil" in verse 10 means calamity, not depravity.

_____

_____

_____

_____

Going Behind the Gates of UZ

Starter: (see above)
Introduction: (see above)
Story Questions: (see above)

Commentary (see the appendixes for an introduction and outline of Job)

Job never really repents, even though some translations use "repent" in the last chapter. The word for repent in the Hebrew language normally means "to turn back" (*shuv*). Eliphaz (22:23) and Elihu (36:10) are the only speakers to use the Hebrew term in the way we interpret repent today. Job uses other words to describe his state of mind after hearing God (42:6). He feels humbled and comforted by coming to grips with the majesty of God for the first time. Job had never really turned away from God. He continued to search for Him despite his confusion over the circumstances. So, in the end, as he sat in the dust and ashes of humility and purification, there was no need for repentance, just acceptance of the fact that the Lord of the universe answers to no one but Himself.

Eliphaz and his friends were a different matter. The Lord firmly rejected their counsel to Job. You might say He held them in contempt of court. They could have received the judgment of Job and suffered the same calamities that he and his family did. But the Lord was gracious unto them and simply called for a sacrifice of repentance (not remorse —the Lord would know the difference). So they went and did as the God of justice and mystery told them to do. To add to their humility, the Lord also directed them to seek Job's prayers. Why Job's prayers? Because Job was a man blameless and upright who feared God (1:1). His prayers were music to the Almighty's ears.

What happened to Elihu? We can only conjecture, but given his station in life at that time and his arrogance, we assume he followed humbly behind Job's friends . . . several paces behind at best and possibly next to Job's wife.

Study Questions

1. The Lord's anger burned against Job's friends, but instead of destroying them with a snap of His fingers, He told them to repent and go on their way. Why? Consider God's words to Ezekiel (Ezekiel 18:32).

_____

_____

_____

2. The Hebrew word for repent means "to turn," but is the emphasis here on turning away from misdeeds or turning to God (Matthew 11:16-20)?

_____

_____

_____

3. What should Job's attitude have been toward his so-called friends (and wife) after they repented (Luke 17:3-4)?

Lifestyle Questions

1. Job may not have needed to repent, but he was awfully confrontational with God (9:13-16). Do you think the Lord wants us to be honest with Him to the point of being rude? What's the limit before we need to repent?

2. If your friends called upon you to turn away from some activity, would you do it? If instead they asked you to seek the Lord in prayer, would you be more likely to follow their advice (Matthew 6:33)?

3. If a person repents, how can we help them continue on the right path? Hint: Psalm 119:11, Galatians 5:16.

NOTES

| 10 |

Vindication Is Sweet

A Book, the Bible, and a Bit of Banter

Starter

Why do we cheer for the underdog, or for someone falsely accused in a movie?

Introduction

Herb Brooks told his 1980 Olympic hockey players, "This team isn't talented enough to win on talent alone," and he was right. The squad was destined to face teams like Sweden, Norway, Czechoslovakia, Russia, and Finland with bigger, faster, and more experienced players. Despite being underdogs all the way, the scrappy bunch of college students believed they could win. They were just about the only ones. The most memorable game was against the Russian army team. No one thought they had a chance to beat the "Big Red Machine." It was a miracle—"the miracle on ice." A final win over Finland vindicated Team USA and Herb Brooks' cantankerous coaching style. They may not have been the most talented or the most elegant group, but their victories proved they were all team.

Story Question

Did Ben's vindication justify all the physical and emotional abuse he took?

Bible Questions

Did Job expect to be vindicated? Then why was he so indignant (13:18, 23:6-7, 13:7-8)?

Going Behind the Gates of UZ

Starter (see above for the question) answer:
Introduction (see above)
Story Question (see above)

Commentary (see the appendixes for an introduction and outline of Job)

There are several stories of vindication in the Bible. Joseph the son of Jacob was cast into prison, accused of accosting Potiphar's wife (Genesis 39:7-20). But God had a plan for Joseph. Through his experience in prison, he rose to rule over all Egypt, second only to Pharaoh. King David was chased by a deranged Saul as if he were a subversive thief seeking the throne of Israel. David could have taken Saul's life (I Samuel 24:3-12) but did not. David was vindicated by Saul's son, Jonathon, who befriended him (I Samuel 20:42), and by his rise to the throne of Israel, which David dedicated to the Lord. Probably the most colorful exoneration comes from the life of Daniel. Daniel was caught praying, which was forbidden, and was thrown into a den of hungry lions. The fact that he survived vindicated him, and he was restored to his position of trust (Daniel 6:7-24). Of course, the greatest story of vindication is Jesus Himself.

In Job's story, he isn't the only one vindicated. If we'd been spectators by the gates of Uz, we might have waited breathlessly to observe one of two events—either a flash of light leaving a small heap of ash where Job had been sitting, or an angel whose touch would heal Job in a flurry of neutrinos. We probably would have been mildly disappointed when the flash did not come despite the convincing arguments by Eliphaz and his friends justifying such an act of God. Like a tragic Greek comedy, Job's saga comes to a happy conclusion.

Who else was vindicated? Certainly not Eliphaz, Bildad, or Zophar. They were marched off to the altar of repentance. Job's wife? Hardly. We know the Adversary had no redeeming qualities. His proposal to draw Job to the dark side failed. So, who else was vindicated? The Lord Himself, of course. Not that He needed it, but in this epic story, He is vindicated on at least two counts. First, His servant Job, whom He expected to remain faithful, went the distance despite his friends and wife. Job thwarted the challenge of the Adversary and through his faith claimed victory. The Lord also found vindication in the poetic heralding of His sovereign position as Creator of the universe and the one who determines what is just. Clearly, He has no requirement to respond to the demands of any created being or court of law.

Study Questions

1. How does Job's vindication compare to that of Ben Calix?

2. Is Job's story about his vindication or the Lord's?

3. How do you think Job's vindication impacted his friends? Were they happy for Job, confused, or full of mixed emotions?

Lifestyle Questions

1. How does forgiveness complement vindication (Nehemiah 9:17)?

2. If we have wrongly judged someone, what should be our attitude toward them after they have been vindicated, and how do we show that?

_____

_____

_____

_____

3. If we are wrongly accused by a loved one, how should we respond? How should we act when we are vindicated?

_____

_____

_____

_____

NOTES

_____

_____

_____

_____

_____

_____

| 11 |

The Promise of New Life

A Book, the Bible, and a Bit of Banter

Starter

What phrase or saying would you like on your gravestone?

Introduction

In the 1966 movie, "The Flight of the Phoenix," a desert sandstorm brings down a Fairchild C82 twin-engine cargo plane. Trapped in the desert with no radio, the crew suffers dehydration, sunburn, starvation, and loss of life, until finally they emerge from the dust and ashes as a new creation on a single engine resurrection of the C82. The strange flying lifeboat, with its passengers on its wings, stays aloft long enough to find a desert oasis and new life for its beleaguered human freight (not aerodynamically feasible—sorry, both Gary and James had to say that).

Like the mythical Phoenix, Ben Calix and Job (who precedes the myth by 1400 years) welcome their demise amid the trials, but rise out of the pit of death to newness of life. In both stories there is a theme of resuscitation and even resurrection. Facing death, they find the promise of new life physically, emotionally, and spiritually.

Story Questions

Why was Ben willing to give up his life for the Company? Was there more to his motive than loyalty to the organization?

Bible Questions

In the story of raising of Lazarus (John 11:38-44), was Lazarus resuscitated or resurrected? What's the difference between resuscitation and resurrection?

Going Behind the Gates of UZ

Starter (see above)
Introduction (see above)
Story Questions (see above)

Commentary (see the appendixes for an introduction and outline of Job)

Scholars disagree about Job's knowledge of the afterlife. He dwells on it and suggests that God can resurrect a person from the pit or Sheol (14:14-15). Sheol equates to Hades in the New Testament. Hades is a place of darkness where the dead wait for the final judgment (Revelation 20:13-14). Job mentions Sheol nine times and Zophar once, but he also mentions the pit, which is a reference to Sheol. Then Elihu (33:18-30) offers a short doctrinal monologue on the subject of Sheol. Here (30:23-24) Elihu presents the concept of a righteous mediator who would ransom a man from death. Is this foreshadowing Jesus' statement that He came to be a ransom for many (Matthew 20:28)? Was the Holy Spirit putting words of promise in Elihu's mouth?

Then we have Job's amazing recounting of redemption unto life (19:23-27). Despite the deterioration of his body (19:26), Job imagines himself restored and standing before God. One can certainly make a resurrection case for Job's prophetic vision of the Lord's power to rescue him from Sheol and restore him in a new body to stand in His presence. Still, other statements by Job suggest that his concept of the resurrection is not well developed, certainly not like Paul's statements in I Corinthians 15.

So, the questions with which scholars grapple are: "Does the suffering of Job present us with a precursor to the doctrine of the resurrection or simply Job's belief that he will be resuscitated in the end, which he was? Is Job's saga just an ancient story similar to Lazarus (John 11:38-44) or Dorcas (Acts 9:40)? Does Job understand that his words in the context of all Scripture represent the promise of a new eternal life (resurrection) or just the promise of a new earthly life (resuscitation)?

These are tough questions, but one thing is for certain—Job and Elihu address the subject of death and life beyond the pit with more hope than might be expected for those who preceded Moses and the prophets.

Study Questions

1. Is Job emphasizing his finite existence or the fact that God was ignoring him when he says, "When a cloud vanishes it is gone, and he who goes to Sheol does not return" (7:9)?

_____

_____

_____

_____

_____

2. Who is Job's redeemer, and how do we know he's not just a referring to a relative (19:25-26)?

3. Could Elihu be asking for a holy messenger (angel) or mediator who can stand in Job's place and offer Himself as a substitute and ransom for Job's transgressions (33:23-34)?

Lifestyle Questions

1. Could a near-death experience be considered a godly resuscitation? Should this be considered a calling of God?

2. How would you use the promise of the resurrection to comfort someone who was suffering? What Scripture verses would you quote? Read I Corinthians 15 and I Peter 1:3.

_____

_____

_____

_____

3. Is the resurrection of the dead a promise of life everlasting (John 5:29)?

_____

_____

_____

NOTES

_____

_____

_____

_____

_____

_____

_____

| 12 |

A Word to the Wise

A Book, the Bible, and a Bit of Banter

Starter

Why is the owl a symbol of wisdom? Find the answer in the *Going Behind the Gates of Uz* starter section.

Introduction

We are inundated today with a flood of data. Many think we're smarter because of the information at our fingertips. That may or may not be true, but does it make us wiser? As Albert Einstein said, "Information is not knowledge." Others have added that knowledge is not wisdom.

Outside the cadet dining hall at the United State Air Force Academy stands a bronze eagle with two fledglings. The statue's quotation reads, "Man's flight through life is sustained by the power of his knowledge" (Austin Miller). This is an inspiring adage meant to greet students full of dining hall "delicacies" as they return to their studies, but the saying falls short of being wise. The last bit should read, "by the power of his knowledge *of God*." Notice we didn't say "knowledge of Scripture." Memorizing Bible verses, or parts of them, can be helpful or harmful.

For example, the Bible says, ". . . there is no God," but the complete verse puts that phrase in the mouth of a fool (Psalm 14:1). Wisdom comes not from memorizing words but rather from the revelation of those words which leads to a relationship with the Almighty. By knowing Him and His nature, knowledge becomes illumination, revealing the wisdom to make right choices—godly choices and goodly choices for our lives and others' lives.

Story Questions

Ben Calix had a lot of information at hand, but did he make wise decisions? Was it wise for him to let Clara bring Otto along? Was it wise to go to Sensen's cabin or Micro's (Dylan's) house?

Bible Question

In 28:28, at the end of the "wisdom chapter," Job says, "Behold, he who fears the Lord—that is wisdom; and to refrain from evil is understanding." What is Job saying?

Going Behind the Gates of UZ

Starter (see question above)

In western culture the owl is the picture of wisdom because of its association with the Greek goddess Athena, the goddess of knowledge and wisdom. In India, however, the owl is the symbol of foolishness, and in southern Africa it's a sign of evil.

Introduction (see above)

Story Questions (see above)

Commentary (see the appendixes for an introduction and outline of Job)

Five books in the Bible come under the heading of "wisdom literature." These books begin with Job, followed by Psalms, Proverbs, Ecclesiastes, and Song of Solomon. Of course, much of the Bible and especially the New Testament could be classified as wisdom literature. Job and his fellow sages reference wisdom and the wise over 30 times. And as one author has said, the book of Job could almost be called a "debate on wisdom." This is primarily due to issues contested in the book like justice, suffering of the innocent, loyalty and faithfulness, and sovereignty. We have covered these themes in previous sections.

Wisdom is not a single faceted jewel. It incorporates experience, knowledge, emotional intelligence, and a consistent set of Judeo-Christian values. Wisdom is not just knowing, it's applying. It's mixing together the knowledge, experience, and values one has collected in life and pouring them into a mold of good judgment. Sitting regally on a tufted pillow and pontificating on the labors and lusts of life is, as Job puts it, nothing but a case of limitless windy words (16:3). To be truly wise you must put on your waders and cast your pearls into the streams of life to see if they lure a weighty catch or sink into obscurity.

Commentators generally refer to chapter 28 as "the wisdom chapter." Job begins his discussion on wisdom by highlighting the fact that many wonders of the earth are readily seen or available like silver and copper, sapphires and gold dust, falcons and lions, and food. Though some rare commodities require long journeys and searching in dark mines, they can be found. Then in verse 12 he gets to his point. "But where can wisdom be found?" He laments that humans don't understand its value and that there is no known source of it in the land of the living. It cannot be bought. Nothing of earthly value is its equal. So, where can people find wisdom? Only the Lord knows the way. Only the one who created the wonders of the world knows its location. It is found in the fear of the Lord and laying aside any departure from His ways (28:28).

The phrase, "the fear of the Lord" is used throughout scripture, but most commonly in the book of Proverbs where it appears 14 times. The writer of Proverbs echoes Job's words as he suggests that the value of wisdom is greater than silver and to be treasured above all else (2:3-6). The author goes on to proclaim that wisdom is found only in fearing and knowing God. This is why the Lord revealed Himself through His prophets and ultimately His appearance on earth as Jesus Christ. So, the Scriptures and prayer become the keys to unlocking the treasure chest of wisdom. For Job, wisdom remained hidden, but today, we have the revelation of God and the illumination of the Holy Spirit to know God's wisdom (I Corinthians 2:12-15).

Study Questions

1. Job suggests that if his friends would be totally silent, they would be considered wise (13:5). Do you agree? When is silence wisdom?

2. Where does wisdom reside on earth? Hint: not in the mind (Proverbs 2:10).

3. Did knowledge or wisdom inform the decision of the 10 spies (and Israelites) whom Moses sent to spy out the land of Canaan? Why was it reasonable but not wise for them to turn back (Numbers 13:17-14:10)?

Lifestyle Questions

1. The opposite of wisdom is foolishness. What are the characteristics of foolish decisions?

2. What sources of "wisdom" in common thought are really uninformed suppliers of folly? Hint: I always check the internet if I'm in doubt—not.

3. Can the revelation of God and the illumination of the Holy Spirit provide the means to make modern-day decisions (Matthew 6:33, II Timothy 3:16)?

APPENDIX I: MATCHING GAME

Match the characters from The Paris Betrayal to the personalities found in Job's saga.

The Paris Betrayal Characters	Job Personalities
1. Ben _____	A. Job's wife
2. Jupiter _____	B. Elihu (the impetuous youth)
3. The Director _____	C. An angel (a guardian)
4. Giselle _____	D. Satan
5. Dylan/Micro _____	E. Bildad (a close friend)
6. Tess _____	F. Eliphaz (the wise elder)
7. Sensen _____	G. One of the Sabeans
8. Clara _____	H. Job
9. Hale _____	I. God
10. The Dutchman _____	J. Zophar (a man of few words)

Answers:

1-H 2-D 3-I 4-A 5-B 6-E 7-J 8-C 9-F 10-G

APPENDIX II: JOB INTRODUCTION AND SUMMARY

Introduction and Background

Job may be the oldest book in the Bible but not the oldest story. Genesis 1-10 certainly outdates the story of Job. Many scholars believe Job to be a contemporary of Abraham or close to it. Five reasons to consider Job to be so old: (1) the author describes Job's wealth as like that of Abraham and Isaac; (2) no priests were mentioned to offer the sacrifices, which predates Moses; (3) Job lived a long time, well over 140 years; (4) Job and his children used an ancient kind of money or silver mentioned only in Genesis, Job, and Joshua.

Job has some unique details. For example, he mentions the constellations of the Bear, Orion, and Pleiades twice (9:9, 38:31-32)—possibly as part of the eastern zodiac of the time. These were well known and particularly beautiful in the heavens of the Middle East. Orion was known as the mighty warrior to the people of Job's time, and the Lord's reference to it in chapter 38 is a play on the human and heavenly imagery. This doubly emphasizes how finite Job was. The Hebrew names of these constellations are *Ash*, *Kesil*, and *Khimah*.

Job also mentions the behemoth (40:15-24) and the leviathan (3:8, 41:1). The writer records a detailed description of the behemoth, which has a similar spelling in ancient Egyptian. Most scholars believe the beast to be a hippopotamus, though some argue that the description of its tail indicates a sauropod. The fact that they are living in the Jordan river adds to the age of Job. As for the leviathan, the original name of this animal and its description led scholars to believe it was a crocodile. Again, there is some disagreement, because the creature is mentioned as breathing fire. Crocodiles are, on the whole, larger than alligators and more aggressive, which may be what is described in chapter 41. Crocodiles were worshiped as powerful gods in ancient Egypt. This is one reason they are referenced by God as an example of worshiping the creation rather than the creator.

Finally, Job may be the first to use "by the skin of my teeth" (19:20). It is a metaphor for being on the brink of death, referring to his emaciated condition and suffering. He is alive but barely.

Theological Summary

Job is one of the books known as wisdom literature in the Old Testament. Job addresses several philosophical themes but is best known for the question: "Why do bad things happen to God's people?" Is God acting justly by letting "evil" happen to anyone, especially the innocent?

Job's self-proclaimed innocence and his suffering serve as the premise for the discussion. In religious studies, this study of justice is referred to as the discipline of theodicy or the vindication of why an almighty God would allow evil (calamity) in the world.

Wisdom (chapter 28) is another theme. It is the key to defeating the Adversary's game plan. Wisdom enables humans to rise above their pain, their humanity, their temptation to curse God, and to humble their finite selves before the Infinite. Of course, this is personified in Job—almost—as a type of Christ who is wisdom and defeats the Adversary (I Corinthians 1:22-24).

Several other themes emerge from the story of Job as he and his "friends" grapple with these topics:

- The innocence or sinfulness of humans
- The lack of justice for those who do evil
- The nature and motives of the Adversary
- Loyalty to and faith in the Creator
- The sovereignty of God to be God independent of human demands
- Friendship in time of need
- Abandonment and the feeling of facing life's pain alone
- The hope of resurrection
- Victory and vindication

NOTES

APPENDIX III: JOB CHARACTER SKETCHES

Job

- A wealthy, righteous, landowner, and family man. Honored in his community for his consistency, integrity, and treatment of others.
- A middle-aged man by the standard of the day (about 70 years old).
- A devout man that offered sacrifices to God even though he was not a priest.
- A man who walked with God despite having no law of Moses to guide him.
- He is a type—a historical forerunner of the Messiah's righteous suffering.
- He is human, a creation of God, who shows frustration with God when there seems to be no reason for his suffering and the suffering of his family.
- In modern day terms, Job is comfortably wealthy (made the right investments in the Market) and is a devout evangelical Christian who worships God daily through personal devotions. He lives his life according to the Word. His world is comfortable, orderly, stable, loving, and predictable. He believes in justice but does not believe God would bring severe calamity upon him without reason.

Job's wife

- Reacts to the situation as anyone would expect a normal human to react.
- Angry at God for the suffering He has brought on her family and angry with Job for not being angry at God.
- In a modern context, you might picture her coming to Job in a light green chenille robe with her hair up in curlers and wearing fluffy pink slippers with a cucumber facial saying, "What more can God do to us before you curse Him and die?"

HaSatan

- "The-Adversary"; in Hebrew "ha" means "the" and "satan" means adversary or accuser. Thus, this is The-Adversary or HaSatan which is all one word in Hebrew.
- A subtle and cunning manipulator intent on depreciating God's glory as Creator and Magistrate of the universe.
- Wants both man and God to suffer for his own discretions by using God's just nature against Him.
- A pitiful being with nothing better to do than bring pain to others. This is characteristic of mankind as well—wishing calamity on others because of their own misfortunes.

Eliphaz

- His name means, "God of fine gold."
- May be an Edomite and descendent of Esau, which would require a slightly later date for the story than Abraham, but his name speaks of an earlier pagan time.
- Came as a friend (2:11) along with Bildad and Zophar.
- Seems to be the leader and probably the eldest and wisest of the trio of friends, possibly older than Job and a trusted adviser.

- He and the others may have come long distances (according to their tribal designations), which would make them more like colleagues (fellow businessmen) in the region.
- He and the others showed compassion and respect for Job's situation (2:11-13).
- Recognized by most commentators as the gentlest and most understanding of the friends.

Bildad

- The meaning of his name is unsure—possibly "not loved."
- A Shuchite—possibly a descendant of Abraham and Keturah (Gen 25:2).
- Less polite to Job, probably because Job did not accept the reasoning of Eliphaz.
- Attacks the character of Job's children and suggests they deserved what they got because of their sins (8:4), which Job disputes in the first chapter, having made sacrifices for them in case they had sinned (1:5).

Zophar

- His name is transliterated *"Tsophar,"* and the meaning of it is uncertain but could be "Chirper" like a bird (Sparrow).
- Probably the youngest of the three friends since he spoke last.
- Quite direct, because he says that he is frustrated with Job's answers.

Elihu

- Elihu means "My God is He."
- The scripture clearly states that he is younger than the rest (Job 32:4, 6).

- Infuriated by the dialogue of the older friends, dying to correct their perspective and their inability to refute Job.
- Takes a different tack in that he claims Job has demeaned God by claiming he is righteous, and therefore Job is undeserving of God's justice.
- Not recognized by God nor chastised by Him as are the other three in God's final comments.

NOTES

APPENDIX IV: JOB OUTLINE

A Brief Annotated Outline of Job

Prologue/Adversary/Job's wife: Chs 1-2

The opening sentence is quite emphatic. Job is that particular man (implying there is no one like him) who is complete/perfect, morally innocent, upright/just, and turns aside from all evil. God shows great pleasure with Job. Job has had a full and pleasing life thus far (wealth, children, property, etc.).

Then in comes the Adversary with the sons of God, and God points to Job, repeating the words of v.1 in v.8. The Adversary claims God has bought Job's affection and righteousness with a comfortable life, implying Job would turn away from God without these comforts. God permits the Adversary to attack Job's family and possessions, but Job blesses the name of the Lord. So, the Adversary again says Job is bribed by his good health, and God permits him to attack Job physically.

Job's wife sums up what should be Job's response and what the Adversary is looking for if Job were an ordinary man; "Do you still hold fast to your integrity [moral innocence]? Curse God and die!" This sets up the moral conundrum. Is Job righteously perfect, or has he intentionally or unintentionally sinned against God? And if he is righteous, how can this be just? Job's friends arrive to console him, supposedly with the wisdom to sort this out.

Job's opening speech

Chapter 3

Job expresses his depression and despair, and eloquently asks, "Why am I not at ease with this?" (3:26). This opens the door for the consolation by his friends to become patronizing.

First round of speeches

Chapters 4-5 Eliphaz

Eliphaz begins by politely reminding Job that he has counseled others and should welcome wisdom from his friends. He points out that all men are made of clay and adversity comes only to those who fall short of innocence. So, accept God's discipline and admit your folly, and He will heal you (5:17-18).

Chapters 6-7 Job

Job responds and proclaims the injustice of his pain. He chastises his friends for abandoning him. He refuses to be silent and claims he is justified to complain in bitterness. Job then turns his words to God and asks, "Have I sinned? What have I done to You, O watcher of men?" (7:20).

Chapter 8 Bildad

Bildad calls Job's words hot air. He suggests that it may have been Job's family who sinned. But in any case, God does not bring calamity on a man for no good reason. If Job would only repent, God will be merciful, and Job will be restored.

Chapters 9-10 Job

Job concedes that there is no one like God and He is beyond questioning (9:12). He points out that God's power is unassailable and no one can take him to court (9:19). Essentially Job has no defense, even if he is righteous and disease (pain & suffering) comes to the just and unjust. Job then dwells in self-pity.

Chapter 11 Zophar

Zophar is a little more direct and thinks that Job is trying to cover his tracks in a pile of words. He also takes offense at Job's attitude. He compares Job to God and quickly points out that there is no comparison. He all but calls Job an empty-headed donkey (11:12). He suggests Job has forgotten his sin or let it slide by without notice. Finally, he beseeches Job to stop protesting and embrace forgiveness and a return to favor.

Chapters 12-14 Job

Job replies that there is nothing new in what they are saying and that their wisdom is the pits—literally the death of wisdom (12:2). Job thinks his friends are mocking him (12:4). Now Job turns on them and calls them dumb as fish (12:8). Job then rehearses several reversals in fortune, which his eyes have seen and his ears understood (13:1). This comes back to Job later when God speaks, and only then does he see the hand of God (42:3-5). Job then calls on his false physicians to be quiet and to listen to his words lest God hold them in contempt. In chapter 14 Job goes into another fit of depression and laments to God.

Second round of speeches

Chapter 15 Eliphaz

Less generous and patient now, Eliphaz calls Job a wind bag full of hot desert air (15:2). Eliphaz is convinced more than before that Job speaks out of guilt and condemns himself with his own words. Eliphaz mocks Job, suggesting he has a secret relationship with God and therefore thinks he is wiser than men older than his father (15:-8-10). Eliphaz suggests that Job has sinned against God by being arrogant and questioning God's actions (15:25). Eliphaz is now convinced that Job deserves what he has gotten and that the emptiness of his life is a sign of his wickedness.

Chapters 16-17 Job

Job suggests his comforters are so pitiful that they should be comforted (16:2). Then he equates them to his persecutors (6:11). Job all but gives up in a deep depression—his spirit is broken (17:1).

Chapter 18 Bildad

Bildad pours salt in Job's wounds by suggesting his depression is a sign of his guilt (18:5, 16, 21).

Chapter 19 Job

On the brink of falling into the abyss of despair, Job entertains the possibility of having gone astray but implies that this is between him and God (19:4). Job has another pity party (19:21), but in the midst of his lament, he comes back to trust in God (19:25-26).

Chapter 20 Zophar

Zophar is indignant, insulted, and says that Job is but a passing dream (or nightmare) and no longer to be remembered.

Chapter 21 Job

Job agrees with Zophar regarding the plight of the wicked but refuses to be corralled with such wicked men as these. Job rises above the counsel of the wicked (21:16).

Third round of speeches

Chapter 22 Eliphaz

Eliphaz becomes a little desperate. He makes up sins that Job must have committed to be suffering under these circumstances. Eliphaz tries one last time to bribe Job with the blessings of God if he will just confess (22:25-26).

Chapters 23-24 Job

Job reiterates his desire to have an audience with God so he can present his case. In an effort to manipulate God (silly Job) by trying to draw Him into defending Himself, Job presents a litany of sins committed by others. These are the ones who should be in Job's shoes and receive God's wrath but have not (Psalm 73). Job then concedes that no one understands the workings of God.

Chapter 25 Bildad

In a terse response, Bildad proclaims that all are born sinners and nothing more than worms and maggots in the presence of God (25:6).

Chapters 26-32:1 Job

Job responds with sarcasm and mocks his comforters. He also acknowledges the depths of the Almighty. He then reasserts his righteousness and that he will not violate the truth to gain favor with God (27:6). Job continues by contending that justice will come to the wicked (ch 27) but asks, "Where is wisdom" and "Who shall find it?" (28:20, 28).

Finally, Job pines for days gone by when he was fulfilled and respected and did good for those around him (ch 29). All that is gone (ch 30, 30:31). Once again, he makes his case for an appearance in the court of the Almighty (31:35). And all are silent. Zophar is speechless.

Elihu's Speaks

Chapters 32:2-37 Elihu

Elihu is to be commended for defending God's goodness and consistency (34:12), but he does it at the expense of Job's righteousness (34:5-6).

Elihu asserts that if you do not find fault with Job, then you are condemning God (34:17), so he builds a case for the honor and impartiality of the Almighty (37:23). Thus, the logic of the three friends is reversed; if God is righteous then Job must be suspect, so "please examine Job in perpetuity, for he answers like a man of iniquity" (34:36).

The Lord Speaks

Chapters 38-42:9 God

In a series of eloquent creation metaphors God puts Job in his place. Job is finite; the Almighty is infinite. Who is Job, the Lord's creation, to instruct the Creator of the universe with all its wonders? The question that sums it all up is, "Where were you when I laid the foundations of the earth? Tell me if you have understanding" (38:4). Job then repents of his impertinence and humbles himself before God (42:1-6).

Finally, God chastises Eliphaz, Bildad, and Zophar and tells them to make sacrifices for their treatment of Job and to atone for their sins. Note that Job is not required to atone for any sin. Strangely, Elihu is not mentioned, nor is the Adversary. Their absence may be considered a silent rebuke, a declaration that God has no esteem for their hubris.

Ch 42:10 Job restored

Job's fortunes are restored twofold, and he lives a full life.

NOTES

APPENDIX V: NOTABLE PASSAGES WORTHY OF DIALOGUE

- Job 1:21a – "Naked I came from my mother's womb, and naked I shall return there."

- Job 1:21b – "The Lord gave and the Lord has taken; may the name of the Lord be blessed."

- Job 2:10b – "'Yea shall we take the good from God and not accept the calamity?' In all this Job did not sin with his lips."

- Job 6:6 – "Can something tasteless be eaten without salt, or is there any taste in the white of an egg?"

- Job 9:25 – "My days are swifter than a runner; they flee without seeing goodness."

- Job 12:17 – "[God] makes counselors walk barefoot [naked] and makes fools of judges" (see Isa 20:4).

- Job 13:3 – "Indeed, I will surely speak to God Almighty [*El Shaddai*], and I will be pleased to present my case to God." An emphatic verse with a rare use of *El Shaddai*—only used five times in the Old Testament (3 in Genesis and 1 other in Ezekiel)

- Job 19:7 – "Behold, I cry, 'Violence!' But I get no answer; I shout for help, but there is no justice."

- Job 19:15 – "Those who live in my house and my maids consider me a stranger. I am a foreigner in their sight."

- Job 19:20b – "And I have escaped only by the skin of my teeth."

- Job 19:25 – "I surely know that my Redeemer lives, and upon the final dust He will take His stand."

- Job 19:26 – "Even after this skin is buried, with my flesh I will behold God."

- Job 23:13 – "But He is unique and who can turn Him? And what His soul [being] desires, that He does."

- Job 28:28 – "And he said to man, 'Behold he who fears the Lord, that is wisdom, and to avoid evil is understanding.'"

- Job 33:4 – "The Spirit of God has made me, and the breath of the Almighty gives me life."

- Job 38:4 – "Where were you when I laid the foundations of the earth? Tell me if you have understanding."

- Job 42:2 – "I know that You can do all things, and that no purpose of Yours can be thwarted."

- Ezekiel 14:20 – "even *though* Noah, Daniel, and **Job** were in its midst, as I live,' declares the Lord GOD, 'they could not deliver either *their* son or *their* daughter. They would deliver only themselves by their righteousness.'"

- James 5:11 – "We count those blessed who endured. You have heard of the endurance of Job and have seen the outcome of the Lord's dealings, that the Lord is full of compassion and *is* merciful."

NOTES

NOTES

NOTES

Dr. Gary C. Huckabay, a graduate of the US Air Force Academy, served as a professor of Old Testament, a chair of biblical studies, a dean at Dallas Baptist University, and president of Williams Baptist College. Dr. Huckabay has contributed to such works as the *Holman Bible Dictionary* and *The Biblical Illustrator*.

Former stealth pilot and fighter pilot James R. Hannibal, also an Air Force Academy graduate, is a three-time Silver Falchion award-winner for his *Section 13* mysteries for kids and a Carol and Selah award-winner for his Clandestine Service spy thrillers. *The Paris Betrayal* is his latest release from Revell Books.

Learn more about Lightraiders discipleship and outreach tools, including the First Watch Scripture memory and application card game with life applications by Dr. Gary C. Huckabay and the Starlots family board game at www.lightraiders.com

www.ingramcontent.com/pod-product-compliance
Lightning Source LLC
Chambersburg PA
CBHW031257290426
44109CB00012B/616